CDB DIK

Gracie Comes Home

THE ADVENTURES OF GRACIE & DIANE

Gracie Comes Home

Written by
Diane Dike, Ph.D.

Forward by
Barbara A. Smith

Illustrated by
Craig A. Grasso &
Samantha A. Grasso
Colorist: Jodi Grasso

*Love
Diane Dike
xoxo*

Part of the profits from the sale of this book will go to support Italian Greyhound rescue groups, such as Rocket Angel Italian Greyhound Rescue.

What does it mean to "rescue" a dog? Why does a dog need to be rescued?
Many people go to pet shops to see the cute puppies. Everyone falls in love with their cute faces and wagging tails. But soon the puppy grows and becomes active and begins to have other needs. Too many times a family is not ready for those things, so they have to give up the puppy. This is where "rescue" comes in. The rescue people help the puppy to find a home where his new family already knows about him and is willing to care for him and love him for who he is. Rescue helps families and puppies find each other.

Gracie and Diane found each other in such a way, and just look at what Gracie can do now! She is a smart and loving dog who got a second chance and in turn has helped her owner to be able to be independent and has given her the ultimate gift— unconditional love. Please ADOPT before you SHOP! Give a rescue dog a "4 ever" home! Search the internet for Greyhound rescue groups in your area.

By Christa Whitaker

A special thank you to Craig, Samantha, and Jodi Grasso for the amazing illustrations found in this book.

A special thank you to Mike Macaluso with Mac Full Service Audio-Visual, for the audio version of this book. mac@macproav.com

ISBN 978-1-932738-45-2
Library of Congress Control Number: 2007932030

First Edition

Printed in the United States

WESTERN REFLECTIONS PUBLISHING COMPANY®

P.O. Box 1149, 951 N. Highway 149 • Lake City, CO 81235
1-800-993-4490 • westref@montrose.net • www.westernreflectionspub.com

Forward

I am so blessed to be grandmother to eight wonderful grandchildren and a new great-granddaughter. My special name is "Mimi!" I treasure the exceptional times we spend together. Many of my fondest memories are of me reading their favorite books at bedtime. I became so acquainted with the story line and characters I would begin to tell my own version. But they were very quick to say, "Mimi, that isn't what the book says!" It was back to reading them word for word.

Bedtime stories have a special place in children's hearts. Their familiarity, happy endings, and the loving voice that reads them give children a sense of security and the knowledge that even though life can be hard, you can get through it. The children's

series, *The Adventures of Gracie and Diane*, offers just such lessons as this sweet and unusual team meet life's challenges with courage, hope, laughter, and faith. I know Gracie and Diane's adventures will become bedtime favorites, too.

Children will identify with Gracie, the Italian Greyhound, who daily makes Diane's life safer. Many people have animals whom they cherish. Our family's favorite was a border collie named Jamie. He was with us for seventeen years, and our children loved him very much. Now, we shower love on Hallie, our son, Michael W., and his family's Golden Retriever.

In the first book of the series, *Gracie Comes Home*, you get to meet my precious friends, Gracie, Diane, and Paul. They have spent time in our home, and the first time we met Gracie she immediately bonded with my husband and me. She would happily jump onto our laps and settle down contently. Paul and Diane, Gracie's "parents," have trained her well, and it is amazing to see how she is in tune to Diane's needs, watching her very carefully all the time.

Years ago we met Diane and Paul in Colorado, and immediately became the best of friends. Before Gracie came into Diane's life, she was often in the hospital. I'll never forget, on one of our trips there, we left her in the hospital in very critical condition, not knowing whether she would survive or not. Diane has a strong faith and a heart for God, and she has inspired so many people. She is filled with joy and love for everyone. Part of that joy comes from the gift she received in Gracie.

God bless each of you as you begin to enjoy *The Adventures of Gracie and Diane* series. *Gracie Comes Home* will leave you anxiously waiting to see what will happen next.

Barbara A. Smith
Author, Friend, and Mother of singing sensation, Michael W. Smith

*Dedicated to my friends, who loved me
when I was broken.*

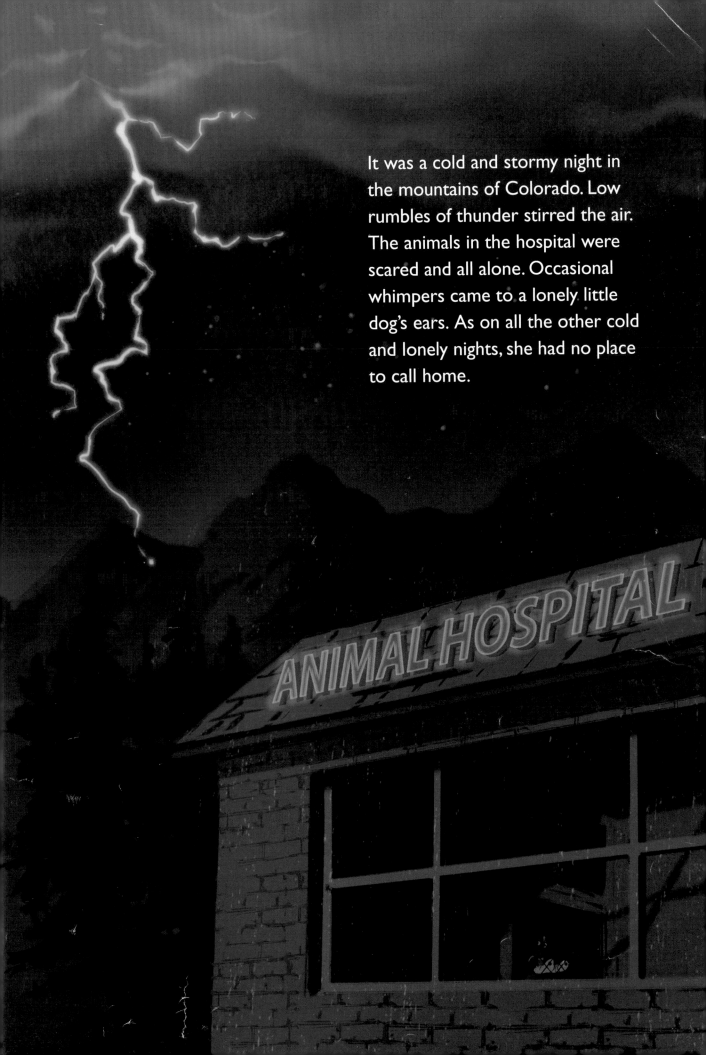

It was a cold and stormy night in the mountains of Colorado. Low rumbles of thunder stirred the air. The animals in the hospital were scared and all alone. Occasional whimpers came to a lonely little dog's ears. As on all the other cold and lonely nights, she had no place to call home.

At almost midnight, she hobbled to the back of her cage. With two broken legs and a broken tail she clumsily wrapped herself into a tiny gray ball. Sniff, sniff!

Rusty, the old bloodhound, asked, "What's the matter, kid?"

The little dog whimpered, "What if no one ever comes for me? What if I never leave this place? What if I can't run or sniff the grass and flowers, again?"

Rusty assured her, "Your day will come. Don't give up hope!"

But she had been there so long even Rusty couldn't be sure her life would ever get better.

The puppy's ears drooped as she cried herself to sleep.

She dreamed of a happier time, in Kansas, where she was born.
She remembered her elegant mother, her energetic father, and
frolicking in the green meadows with her brothers and sisters.
Suddenly, her dream came to an end with a loud thunderclap.

Meanwhile, just across town, Diane was very sick with an incurable disease. Her husband, Paul, was on a fishing trip, and the rain made her feel sad and lonely. She said a prayer. "Lord, is there a little puppy dog out there who needs me as much as I need her? If there is, please show me where she is, if it is Your will."

The next morning Diane got a call that would change her life forever. A friend called and told Diane about an injured puppy at the animal hospital. Diane was so excited she went

The little dog felt the room whirling around her as she started to wake. "Where are you taking me?" the puppy thought as the doctor handed her to a stranger.

She was scooped into two loving arms. "Mmmm, the beautiful lady smells like a daisy." The lonely little dog snuggled in.

"Hi baby doll, my name is Diane."

Her voice was soft like an angel's and her smile as bright as the morning sun.

The puppy's heart melted like butter in a hot pan.

The doctor told Diane, "Her owner abandoned her when she got injured. No one wants to adopt a broken dog, and I don't know if I can fix her. She may never be able to run and play."

The little dog's head drooped.

The doctor sighed. "Do you want her?"

The little dog held her breath. "Please say yes!"

"Hmm," Diane thought to herself. "A dog is a big responsibility, yet I did pray for you ...Yes! May I take her home now?"

The little dog looked into Diane's joyful eyes. Happiness filled her, too, and she wagged her broken tail with love! "Arf! Arf! Yippee! I'm going home!"

The doctor shook his head sadly, "It's too soon to take her home."

Diane didn't want to leave her new friend, who snuggled closer, seeming to feel the same.

Diane held her close. With determination she said, "Don't you worry. I will be back tomorrow, and the next day, and the next, until I can bring you home."

The little dog couldn't believe it when Diane handed her back to the doctor. "No, wait!"

Diane whispered, "Take good care of her, she's my baby now."

Clunk! The door closed. The puppy watched Diane out the window until she couldn't see her anymore. Back to her cold sad cage she went.

Diane couldn't look back.

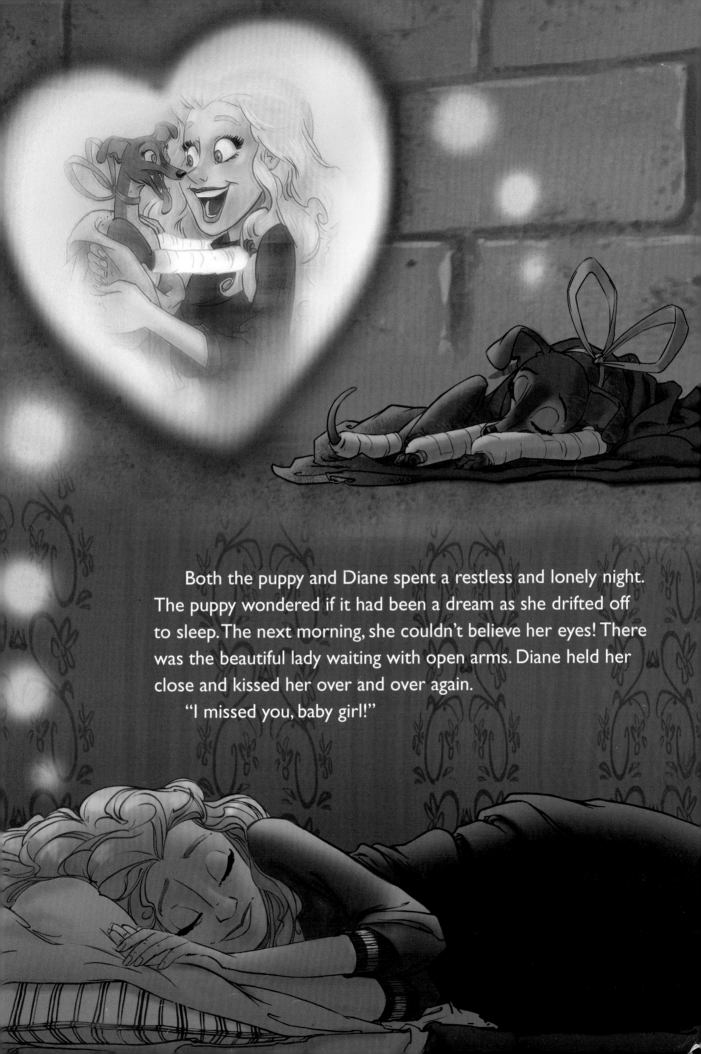

Both the puppy and Diane spent a restless and lonely night. The puppy wondered if it had been a dream as she drifted off to sleep. The next morning, she couldn't believe her eyes! There was the beautiful lady waiting with open arms. Diane held her close and kissed her over and over again.

"I missed you, baby girl!"

Diane carried her outside. The puppy panted with excitement. Everything seemed new and fun, but when Diane put her down, the grass prickled her delicate feet. "Ow! Ow!" she thought, but didn't make a sound.

"You need a name," Diane declared.

"Happy seems like a good name." Then, it came to her. "Gracie! That will be your name because you are my gift from God." Diane giggled, "Even with casts on, you walk so gracefully."

Gracie's ears perked up with approval when she heard her new name.

While Diane watched Gracie play,
cars zoomed, bumblebees buzzed,
squirrels scrambled up the trees, and
Diane sang to Gracie.

Gracie gave Diane tiny, wet
kisses and pranced around the park.
Watching her play happily, Diane
realized she was happy, too.

Their bond of friendship grew with each visit. Because of her illness, Diane knew how it felt to be broken, scared, and alone. When Diane couldn't walk, her husband, Paul, like a knight in shining armor, carried her or pushed her in her wheelchair. Diane knew just what to do to help Gracie heal.

When Paul returned from his fishing trip, Diane told him about Gracie.

He said, "Oh, don't be silly. I've never had a dog and I don't want a dog. What are we going to do with a broken dog?"

Diane gripped Paul's arm, "You've got to meet Gracie."

He finally agreed.

The next day Diane's heart was pounding as she and Gracie waited for Paul in the park near the animal hospital. Several people stopped to ask about Gracie's broken legs. Diane told everyone her story. When she shared that Paul hadn't met Gracie but was on his way, everyone decided to wait to see his reaction.

Soon, Paul came walking toward them. Diane gasped, "Here he comes!"

Everyone clapped and cheered.

Paul, startled to see so many people, smacked his head and sighed, "Oh, no!"

With a soft, shaky voice, Diane said, "Paul, this is Gracie."
All was silent. Gracie, gathering her strength, limped right
over to Paul. She picked up her legs and placed them on
Paul's knees, then looked at Paul with her gentle brown eyes.

Looking down at Gracie, Paul couldn't stop himself. "Okay, you can have the dog!"

Everyone in the crowd cheered and clapped all the louder.

After Paul and Diane said goodbye to the crowd, Paul became very serious.

"I am thankful to see you happy, but what if Gracie's legs never work? What if she can't walk again?"

"Then I'll carry Gracie all the days of her life," Diane cried. "Just like you carry me, when my legs don't work."

Paul hugged Diane. With tears in his eyes, Paul said, "Let's take Gracie home!"

Before they could take her, they needed to talk to the doctor.

Gracie's chest swelled with pride as she hobbled over to share her good news with Rusty. "Kid, I couldn't be happier for ya. Don't know when our paths will cross again. Ah, shucks, I'm gonna miss ya," Rusty howled. Slobbering all over Gracie, Rusty moaned, "I'm proud of ya, kid, now get on out of here."

"Thanks for everything, Rusty! You've been a good friend." Gracie sniffed and kissed him goodbye.

"Now listen carefully." The doctor gave his orders. "You must keep Gracie safe, only let her walk a little, and never leave her alone."

"We'll take good care of her, we promise," chimed Paul and Diane. Diane reached toward Gracie, and she sprung into Diane's arms. They kissed each other gleefully. With the adoption papers signed, Paul, Gracie, and Diane became a family.

"We'll always be together, won't we, um, Mother?" Gracie sighed sheepishly. The word "Mother" filled her heart with thanksgiving.

"I'll love you forever," Diane crooned. And she danced Gracie around.

When they got home, Gracie pranced around her new toys and bowls full of water and food. She sniffed everything enthusiastically, then twirled a couple of times and settled on top of it all. Gracie felt like a princess.

Diane lay down next to Gracie. As they snuggled side by side they took a long nap, dreaming of the amazing adventures that lay ahead. Diane awakened and suddenly realized Gracie was helping her feel better. Diane wondered if someday Gracie could become her service dog...

But, that's another story.

For now, Gracie and Diane say, "See you on the next adventure. Be careful and be kind!"

The End

About the Author

Diane Dike, Ph.D. is a motivational and educational speaker, singer, and author. She is also a passionate, successful and gifted teacher, therapist and friend. Diane lives in the Vail Valley of Colorado with her husband and, of course, Gracie, her rescued Italian Greyhound service dog. Diane has a BA in Physical Education, Recreation and Health with a Minor in Theology. She also has a Masters equivalent in Behavior Disorders and a Ph.D. in Human Services. She started her own ministry, "Dr. D. Ministries" in Florida where she ministered to prisoners, the elderly, and to students. She began an "Adopt a Grandparent" program, teaming young people with seniors. She did public relations work for McDonald's, creating outstanding programs in support of her community. She has volunteered and spoken for "Habitat for Humanity," to many churches and conferences, and traveled with some of the biggest names in Christianity as a massage therapist and prayer warrior. She was the star singer in the laser shows at Cypress Gardens for several seasons. She also taught Pre-kindergarten special needs children as well as students up to the University level. For more information about Diane Dike and Second Chance with Saving Grace, go to www.DianeDike.com.

About the Illustrators

Craig A. Grasso: "I was looking for an opportunity to use my gifts and talent for the Lord. The next thing I knew, He sent me this endearing story and the opportunity I needed to serve Him," said Craig.

Craig discovered his talent at a young age. After four years in the Army and fathering two beautiful children, Craig returned to college where he received his Bachelor of Fine Arts degree in Illustration. Upon graduation, Craig worked freelance for a comic strip and created illustrations for children's books. Craig has worked on many hit animated feature films including: *Ice Age II, Brother Bear, Lilo and Stitch,* and *Mulan.* He currently works as a member of the story team for Pixar.

Craig has four daughters and a son and lives with his wife and three daughters in the East Bay area of San Francisco. "This book shares the love of God. I am proud to be a part of it and am thrilled to share this experience with my talented daughter, Samantha," Craig stated with a smile.

Samantha A. Grasso: "Samantha Grasso is relatively fresh in the illustration world, but her talent exhibits ability far beyond her years," said Jodi Grasso who worked with Samantha on the book, *Gracie Comes Home.* Upon graduation from college, Hallmark® wisely snatched up Samantha and put her on staff as an illustrator. Samantha also does illustrations for bands, graphic designers, and friends. She enjoys extending her talent as a singer and songwriter with her band. An avid Christian, Samantha humbly volunteers much of her time to local youth and those in need.

Backward

Gracie Comes Home represents an amazing story that shares a message of hope. Everyone wants a place to call home—where people love us and accept us no matter what. Diane Dike provided a warm and loving place for Gracie in her home and in her heart.

As I look back upon many years of friendship with Diane, I am overwhelmed with joy and happiness as I realize Diane has done the same thing for me. Diane is a forever friend, always there with a word of encouragement, a helping hand or a powerful prayer. She often finishes our phone calls with, "Stay strong and courageous, you mighty woman of God!"

God has provided Diane with Gracie to help improve the quality of her life and help her to stay strong and courageous. They have many heartwarming tales to share. I can see their delightful series becoming a favorite for animal lovers of all ages.

In spite of the seriousness of Diane and Gracie's afflictions and, because of them, they are a beautiful example of overcoming. They inspire me to do the same. I hope you enjoy the portrait of Gracie I created for Diane.

Through our pilgrimage on Earth it is a rare opportunity to meet someone like Diane. Everywhere she goes people stop her to ask about little Gracie and she patiently answers all their questions. Now this beautiful book will tell their unique story so Diane can get her shopping done quicker, so she can get home and rest. Through their stories you will see that we all matter and can make a difference for the good, through laughter and tears, if we will take the time to care. And when we do, it can change our lives forever.

So buckle up as the fun has just begun! I look forward to the next edition of, *The Adventures of Gracie and Diane* and I know you do too!

Andrea Roth-Moore
World famous Artist, www.dazzlecreekstudio.com